To the Nichols,

Thank you for caring about people with
AIDS. Best wishes.

Lynda Arnold
11/16/98

My Mommy Has AIDS

Written by

Lynda Arnold

Illustrated by Students from
Rosemont School of the Holy Child

Proceeds from the sale of this book benefit:
National Campaign for Healthcare Worker Safety
Elizabeth Glaser Pediatric AIDS Foundation
The National Pediatric and Family HIV Resource Center
Camp Heartland

Dream Publishing

For my family with love

Dream Publishing
P.O. Box 1645
Blue Bell, PA 19422

Copyright © 1998 by Lynda Arnold

Designed by Penelope C. Paine
Edited by Gail M. Kearns
Typesetting by Cirrus Design

Text illustrations by students in grades 2-5 from Rosemont School of the Holy Child

Publisher's Cataloging-in-Publication
(Provided by Quality Books)

Arnold, Lynda.
My Mommy has AIDS / by Lynda Arnold ; [designed by Penelope Paine ;
edited by Gail M. Kearns ; illustrations by Ellen M Monahan and the students
at the Rosemont School of the Holy Child]. — 1st ed.
  p. cm.
ISBN 1-892073-01-3
SUMMARY: In simple language, young David explains to his peers what AIDS
and HIV infections are, and how his family uses music, laughter, and love
to cope with his mother's illness.
1. AIDS (Disease)—Juvenile literature. 2. Children of AIDS patients—Juvenile literature.
3. HIV infections—Juvenile literature. 4. AIDS (Disease)—Patients—Juvenile literature.
I. Rosemont School of the Holy Child (Rosemont, Pennsylvania) II. Title.

RC607.A256A76 1998   616.97'92 [E]
                                      QBI98-429

Manufactured in Hong Kong

A Note to Adults

This book is designed to be read by adults to young children ages four to eight. Some children may be able to handle more in-depth facts and information about HIV/AIDS. For these children, and adults, too, there is a list of additional resources and reading material available at the end of this book.

The information contained in this book is presented in a story format and reflects the facts we have about HIV/AIDS at the time of this publication. Since research in the AIDS field changes quickly, there may be new findings not mentioned in this publication. Therefore, it is important for each and everyone of us to keep abreast of what is taking place in the area of AIDS.

Hello! My name is David. I like to play baseball, race my cars and ride my bike. My family is just like any other family you know. Maybe we live on your block or go to your school.

This is my sister Ashley. She's my best friend. We play tag and hide-and-seek together. We especially like to go out for ice cream cones. Strawberry is my favorite flavor. Ashley usually picks chocolate chip.

We live with our mommy and
daddy and our dog, Sparky.
Daddy fixes computers and
mommy is a nurse. When I get
sick, mommy takes good care
of me. Pretty soon I feel better.
I think mommy is a great nurse!

Sometimes mommy gets more sick than any of us. She has been sick for a very long time. Mommy has a disease called AIDS. That stands for acquired immune deficiency syndrome. That's kind of hard to say, but mommy says it means that she can't fight germs like I can.

I learned all about AIDS from talking to my mommy and daddy. I am a real good listener, and I always ask questions. When I start to cry, mommy hugs me and holds me tight. She understands that talking about AIDS can sometimes make me sad. When mommy starts to cry, I make her laugh. We are a great team.

Having AIDS is like having a really bad cold or flu that never goes away.

Anyone can have AIDS. You can be a grown-up or a kid. You can be black or white. You can be any color at all. People with AIDS live in every neighborhood, city and country in the world. They go to school, work and church. They take vacations just like everybody else.
They even like to play sports and go to movies, just like you and me.

Some kids and grown-ups don't know anything about AIDS. They might even be scared to sit next to mommy or shake her hand. These people have the wrong idea about how you get AIDS. Just look at me, or Daddy, or Ashley. We are not scared of mommy. We still give her lots of hugs. We are smart about AIDS.

AIDS is first caused by a virus called HIV, that stands for human immuno-deficiency virus. When someone gets the HIV virus they are not sick right away. Some people live with the HIV virus for a very long time without ever getting AIDS. Most people, though, will get sick. Their heads might hurt, and they might have trouble breathing or get tired very easily. I think the worst part about AIDS is that right now there is no cure. Many people with AIDS have already died.

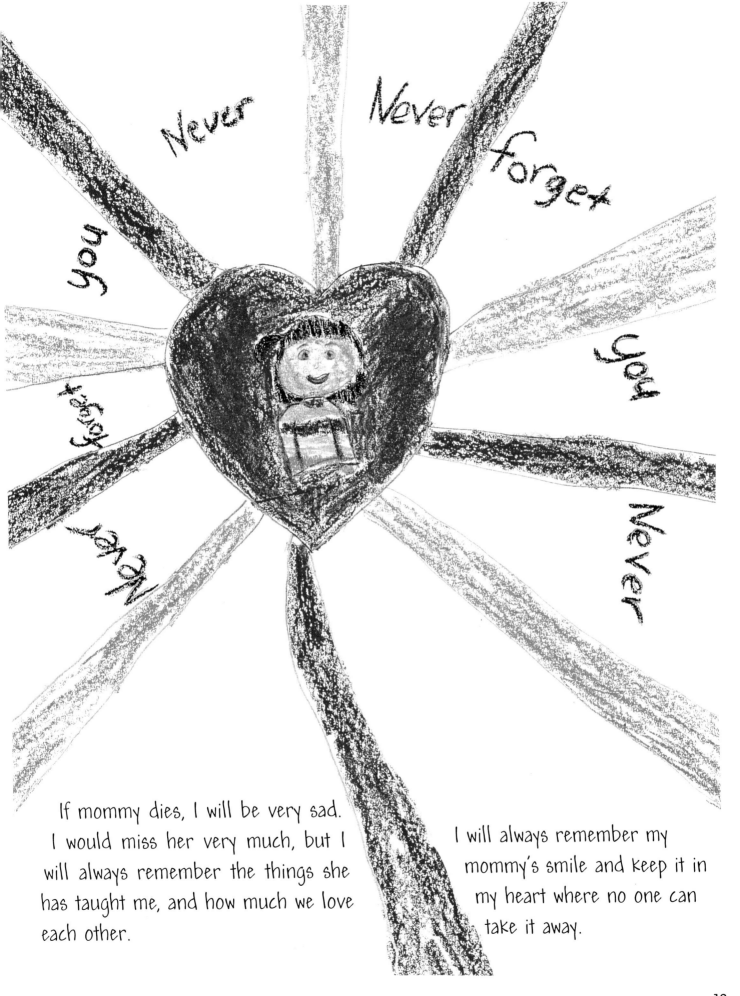

Never Never forget you

you forget Never Never

If mommy dies, I will be very sad. I would miss her very much, but I will always remember the things she has taught me, and how much we love each other.

I will always remember my mommy's smile and keep it in my heart where no one can take it away.

People like my mommy can do lots of things to help them live longer. They can eat lots of fruits and vegetables, go to bed early, wash their hands and take all their medicine. This will help their bodies to stay strong and healthy. Ashley and I eat lots of fruits and vegetables, too. Mommy says that they are as good for us as they are good for her.

Even though there is no cure, people with AIDS take lots of medicine. Mommy's pills are all different colors. There are big ones that look like tiny eggs. There are little ones that look like peas. Once in a while, mommy even gets medicine through a needle in her arm.

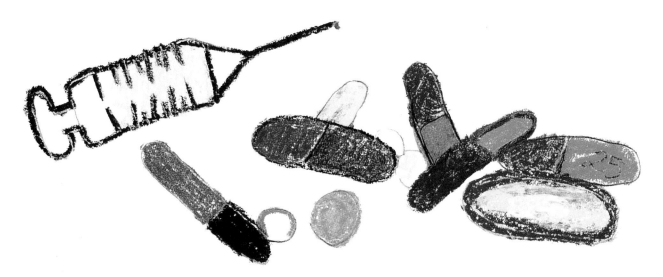

Mommy has lots of friends who have AIDS. Some are doctors and teachers, athletes and movie stars. Others are bus drivers and mail carriers. Some are children and teenagers. There are even babies with AIDS. They got the HIV virus while growing inside their mommy. Not all moms with AIDS have babies with AIDS, but some do.

Sometimes Ashley and I go with mommy when she visits the doctor. We hold her hand so that she is not scared, and we always sing silly songs to make her laugh. Sometimes the doctor sings with us! That makes Ashley and me laugh too.

Mommy wants everyone to know that
people with AIDS can look just like
her, or daddy, or Ashley, or me.
They could look just like you. Do you
know someone with AIDS? Do you
love them a whole lot? Mommy says
there's no reason not to love them.

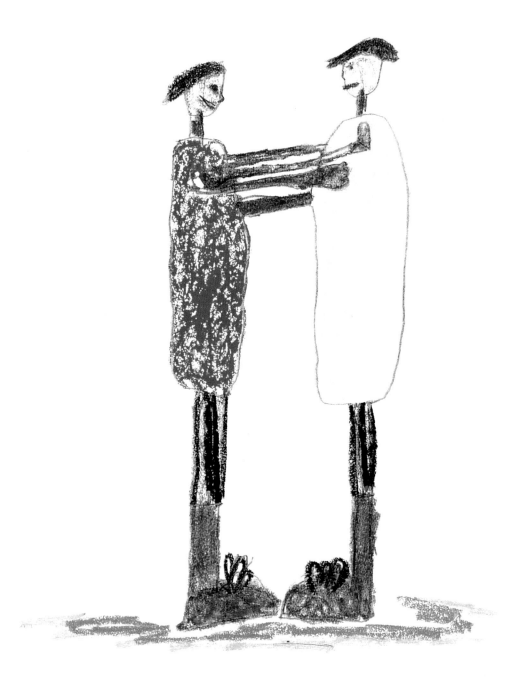

It is very important to be friends with people you know and love who
have AIDS. Even if they feel sick, you can still show them how much you
love them.

You can make them laugh and smile, give them a big hug or draw them a special picture. Don't ever make fun of them. That wouldn't be nice and it might hurt their feelings.

Some people may not even know they have AIDS. You have to get a special test from your doctor to see if you have the AIDS virus. It's a good idea to get the test done because if you are not careful you could give AIDS to someone you love.

AIDS is not an easy disease to catch. The HIV virus is found mostly in people's blood and sometimes in other body fluids. Most people get AIDS because they forget how to be safe around someone else's blood.

To be safe from AIDS you should never touch other people's blood. You should never share razors, scissors, needles or toothbrushes.

You should always get a grown-up when someone gets hurt with a cut or a scrape.

It's okay to hug, hold hands, dance, eat or ride the bus with someone who has AIDS. You can swim in the same pool, live in the same house and even use the same bathroom. You won't get AIDS from a bug bite or any animal. The virus is not spread that way.

Someday there will be a
cure for AIDS. I hope that day
comes really soon! Then mommy
and daddy and all our friends will be
very, very happy! Goodbye medicine,
goodbye tears, goodbye pain and
goodbye fears!
(Hello hopes and dreams and smiles!)

Until that special day, goodbye friend! Remember to be smart about AIDS. Remember to be safe. Talk to your teachers, parents and friends about AIDS. Ask lots of questions. Always be kind to someone with AIDS.

My mommy says that if everybody is smart, safe and nice about AIDS, then our world will be a happier and healthier place to live!

I think mommy's right. What do you think?

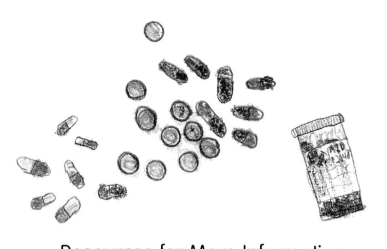

Resources for More Information

You can obtain further information about HIV/AIDS from the following associations and foundations:

The National AIDS Hotline
1-800-342-AIDS

The CDC/National AIDS Clearinghouse
for Publications
P.O. Box 6003, Dept G
Rockville, MD 20850
Tel: (800) 458-5231

Elizabeth Glaser Pediatric AIDS
Foundation
1311 Colorado Avenue
Santa Monica, CA 90404
Tel: (310) 395-9051
www.pedaids.org
Identifies, funds and conducts research for
the prevention of maternal HIV/AIDS

National Association of People with AIDS
1413 K Street NW
Washington, DC 20005
Tel: (202) 898-0414
www.thecure.org

Mothers' Voices
165 West 46th Street, Suite 701
New York, NY 10036
Tel: (212) 730-2777

The National Pediatric and Family HIV
Resource Center
UMDNJ 30 Bergen Street
ADMC # 4
Newark, NJ 07103
Tel: (800) 362-0071
Tel: (973) 972-0410
Fax: (973) 972-0399
www.kidsconnect.org

Camp Heartland
3326 East Layton Avenue
Cudahy, WI 53110
1-800-724-HOPE
World's only year round camping conference
and respite center for children infected and
affected by AIDS
www.campheartland.com

Caring For Babies With AIDS
P.O. Box 351535
Los Angeles, CA 900035
Tel: (213) 931-9828
Residential home for infected children ages
newborn through eight

The NAMES Project Foundation
Sponsor of the AIDS Memorial Quilt
310 Townsend Street, Suite 310
San Francisco, CA 94107
Tel: (415) 882-5500
Fax: (415) 882-6200
E-mail: info@aidsquilt.org
Website: www.aidsquilt.com

National Campaign for Healthcare Worker
Safety, Inc.
3108 Jolly Road
Norristown, PA 19401
Tel: (610) 279-1632
Tel: (800) 936-7370
Fax: (610) 279-1304
Website: www.healthcaresafety.com

Ryan White Foundation
1717 West 86th Street, Suite 220
Indianapolis, IN 46260
Tel: (800) 444-RYAN or (317) 876-1100
Website: www.ryanwhite.org

National Minority AIDS Council
1931 13th Street NW
Washington, DC 20009-4432
Tel: (202) 483-6622

Other Books to Read:

AIDS: First Facts for Kids
by Linda Schwartz
(Grades 4-6)
The Learning Works, Inc.
P.O. Box 6187
Santa Barbara, CA 93160
Tel: (800) 235-5767
Fax: (805) 964-1466

AIDS: Answers to Questions Kids Ask
by Barbara Christie-Dever
(Grades 6-8)
The Learning Works, Inc.
P.O. Box 6187
Santa Barbara, CA 93160
Tel: (800) 235-5767
Fax: (805) 964-1466

AIDS: What Teens Need to Know
by Barbara Christie-Dever
(Grades 9-12)
The Learning Works, Inc.
P.O. Box 6187
Santa Barbara, CA 93160
Tel: (800) 235-5767
Fax: (805) 964-1466

Dream Publishing

P.O. Box 1645
Blue Bell, PA 19422 USA

Available from Dream Publishing

Angels of Love — Celebrating Diversity and Adoption. A children's story that encourages dialogue about adoption, ethnic diversity and the values of love, compassion and understanding which help to strengthen every family unit. Appropriate for young children ages 3-9 years. $18.95/ U.S. dollars each

My Mommy Has AIDS. In this story, young David explains in simple terms about HIV/AIDS and how his family deals with his mother's illness with care and love. Appropriate for children ages 3-9 years. $18.95/ U.S. dollars each

A Higher Standard: The Lynda Arnold Story Highlights Lynda Arnold's story and other personal stories of occupational exposure and infection surrounding needlestick injuries. Discusses preventative issues and possible solutions to the problem. (VHS 40-minute video documentary) $49.95/ U.S. dollars each

Telephone orders: (800) 936-7370 or (610) 279-7439

On-line orders: www.healthcaresafety.com

More Information: (800) 936-7370 or (610) 279-7439
Fax (610) 279-1304

Special Thanks

I would like to thank the faculty, parents and students at Rosemont School of the Holy Child for their time, talent and commitment to this project. This school excels in education and Christian philosophy. The love and energy with which each child is surrounded helps to foster and guide personal growth, values, strength and community-based action. As a proud graduate, I eagerly sing your praises. I only wish that every child could grow with such openness and support. With AIDS education programs like yours, children at an early age can and do learn about prevention of HIV/AIDS and how to be compassionate toward those with the illness.

Class of 2004	Class of 2003	Class of 2002	Class of 2001	
Christopher	Kelly	Meghan	Lauren	Casey
Matthew	Lindsay	Jacquelyn	Andrew	Marie
Peter	Timothy	Kathleen	Elizabeth	Alison
Kaitlin	Caroline	Gregory	Chelsea	Alexander
Nailah	Stephanie	Kathryn	Kerry	Kelly
Regina	Christopher	Hannah	Paige	Ryan
Elizabeth	Kevin	Catherine	Nicole	Ricky
Timothy	Michael	Nicholas	Stephan	Robert
Caroline	Colin	Tory	Patrick	Jessica
Katherine	Francis	Daniel	Andrew	Lara
Gretchen	Grace	Joseph	Alexandra	Giuliana
Juliann	Caitlin	Stephanie	Matthew	Logan
James	William	Thomas	J. P.	Christopher
Christopher	Daniel	Meghan	Elizabeth	Daniel
Colleen	Bridget	Lauren	Danielle	Christine
Stephen	Robert	Nicole	Jamie	Christopher
Erringer	Meghan	William	Hillary	
Madeline	Christopher	Paul	Ryan	
John	Mary Lauren	Bryan	Michelle	
Marisa	Meghan	Robert	Thomas	
Katherine	Erik	Rosemary	Katie	
Kristine	Eugenia	Brendan	Kristen	
Nicholas	Allegra	Daniel	Amy	
Mary Ann	Piervincenzo	James	Michael	
	Kelly	Stephen	Brian A.	
	James	Mariana	Patrick	
	Adriana	Emily	Brendan	
	William	Kate	Kelly	

And my appreciation and thanks go to Lucy Hening, Ellen Monahan and Padma Nolt for their contributions and expertise.

Acknowledgment

For my family and friends, I thank you for your love and dedication. Without your support, this book and the very real story of life and love after HIV infection would never have been told.

To men, women, parents, grandparents, children and young adults everywhere who themselves are HIV positive or have AIDS, we celebrate your lives with this book. We acknowledge that the struggle against AIDS is not over and that education remains a very real and powerful weapon against being infected by the HIV virus.

This book is particularly dedicated to all mothers whose stories of HIV infection or AIDS have never been told. May you find health, joy, love and support. May those who have died find eternal peace and may your families have strength, understanding and hope.

Finally, to my husband Tony, and our children, David and Ashley, I LOVE YOU. Each of you fills my heart with such joy and pride. You make every day a constant gift to me. You are my angels. Together we will always have love. Together we wait and pray for a cure.